AF438012

Faerie Magick for Beginners

Immersive Magic, Volume 3

Merryl Kowalska

Published by Merryl Kowalska, 2022.

While every precaution has been taken in the preparation of this book, the publisher assumes no responsibility for errors or omissions, or for damages resulting from the use of the information contained herein.

FAERIE MAGICK FOR BEGINNERS

First edition. December 11, 2022.

Copyright © 2022 Merryl Kowalska.

ISBN: 979-8215053164

Written by Merryl Kowalska.

Also by Merryl Kowalska

Immersive Magic
A Guide to Acquiring an Astral Magic Wand
Solitary Witchcraft for Beginners
Faerie Magick for Beginners

Table of Contents

For Angelica

Introduction

Immersive Magic: Faerie Magick for Beginners is a magical manual that teaches the secret art of faerie magick. Faeries, also spelled as *fairies*, are magical creatures. There is so much that you can learn from them, and they can be wonderful allies on your magical journey. I have been practicing faerie magick for more than 13 years, and I am now about to teach you all that I have learned. The teachings that you are about to learn came from my own personal experience, established magical knowledge, as well as from the wisdom that I received from my mentor, Witch K.

Faerie magick has existed for so long that some magical practitioners believe that it is as old as mankind. It is about working magick with the faerie creatures. Faeries are very much learned in the art of magic. They are naturally magical beings. It is not uncommon for witches and wizards to have the guidance and help of a fae from time to time. In fact, there are magical practitioners who specialize primarily on building a good relationship with faerie creatures. This way, they know that they have a powerful team that they could call whenever needed.

Immersive Magic: Faerie Magick for Beginners teaches the essential teachings and principles of faerie magick. You will also learn practical techniques and exercise to allow you to practice this ancient magical craft. The good news is that faerie magick is not a difficult magical practice, as long as you know the right steps to take. This book is written in a simple, direct, and easy-to-understand format, so that you can focus completely on learning and experiencing the beauty of faerie magick.

It is also noteworthy that the practice of faerie magick will allow you to develop your overall magical faculties and abilities. It will also give you a deeper sense of spirituality since you will be dealing with spiritual beings. Indeed, there is so much that you can learn from this magical art. Just give it a try and see how it works for you. Do not worry; it is safe, and you can always turn around and walk away if you ever change your mind.

Imagine the wonders that you can do once you have a faerie friend to help you. You can even have multiple faerie friends, if you want. Indeed, if you want to truly experience what a magical life is all about, then this is the magic for you.

Are you ready to learn the secrets of faerie magick? If yes, then welcome into this amazing world of faerie—where there is goodness and peace, imagination and mysteries, a place where magic comes alive.

What is a Faerie?

A faerie is a creature of magick. When people think of faeries, they would probably imagine a small, winged-creature that can do wonderful magic. Well, they are not far from the truth. Faeries are, indeed, magical beings. However, faeries may or may not have wings, and their size may vary; there are small faeries, but there are also huge faeries, even bigger than humans. But, yes, they do work real magic, and this is for sure.

Faeries are nature spirits who, according to legends, used to be in close contact and open communication with humans. However, humans became bad and evil as greed and sin entered their hearts, and so the faeries gradually withdrew until we could no longer see them anymore, except only in some exceptional cases.

It should be noted that faeries are pure creatures of magic. For the faeries, magic simply flows and happens naturally. It is like breathing for them. However, unlike humans that are composed of all the four elements of nature (fire, water, air, and earth), faeries do not have all the four elements. Most of the time, they are limited to one element only; hence, they are also called *elemental spirits*. Some faeries do have up to three elements, but you will mostly find fae creatures to be made of just a single element only.

Fae creatures might be elusive to humans these days, but there are many of them who take interest in humans who practice the magical arts. Therefore, as a magical practitioner, this works to your advantage as it means that they are more likely to reveal themselves to you.

You must also understand that faeries have freewill, and their level of intelligence also varies. There are fairies that are very smart, but there are also those that are known for being dumb—and I mean very dumb. In this regard, it can be said that fairies and humans are alike. However, unlike humans who inhabit a physical form, faeries exist and live in the astral dimension. But, this does not mean that they are separate from us. It is a long-established teaching in occult sciences that the physical realm and the astral realm coexist with each other, and they affect each other. Therefore, do not think of faeries as being irrelevant or disconnected from the human world.

Many faeries these days are cautious of humans. It is believed that we used to live side by side with them, but evil entered the hearts of men, and that was when faeries started to avoid us. Nevertheless, there are still faeries out there who love to meet and even make friends with humans, especially if you are a practitioner of magic. However, there are also faeries who would do their best to stay away from all humans. To deal with these faeries, you must approach them in the right way. You will know more about this later in this book.

Faerie magic is about doing magic with the faeries. The objective is to meet and successfully befriend a faerie. Having faeries as friends can be a really helpful magical ally that could help you with your magical work, whatever it may be.

Now that you know know more about the fae beings, it is time to head to our next subject: meditation.

Meditation Practice

Before you actually start working with faeries, it is important that you have the right state of mind. It is a well-established teaching in magic that all true and most genuine magic starts and ends in the mind. Indeed, your state of mind is very important when doing any form of magical work. The best way to acquire the right mindset is through the practice of meditation.

There are people who feel intimidated when they encounter the word *meditation*. However, there is really nothing for you to feel intimidated or worry about. In fact, the practice of meditation is very easy; and, it is actually more about not doing anything rather than requiring you to do something. It is more about relaxation and clearing the mind rather than doing specific acts.

The best and only way to know what meditation really is about (and just how easy and natural it is) is through real and personal practice/experience. Having said that, here are the steps:

Assume a comfortable position and relax. Close your eyes, and do not think about anything. In this meditation, you are going to use the mantra, *Maranatha*. The word *Maranatha* is in Aramaic, the language that is believed to have been spoken by Jesus Christ when he walked the earth. *Maranatha* means *Come, Lord, come, Lord Jesus.*

Begin to say your mantra: *Maranatha*. Say it lovingly, gently, and repeatedly. You may say it verbally or in your mind only. The way I like to do it is by saying it verbally for about a minute or two, and then I slowly shift to saying it mentally.

As you say your mantra, gently focus on it in exclusion of all other thoughts. If thoughts continue to arise in the mind, ignore them. Only focus on your mantra, and do not think about anything else. If you catch yourself wandering off away from the mantra at any time, simply return to your mantra ever so gently.

Be one with your mantra, and let go of everything else. Relax, meditate, and let go.

At any time that you want to end this meditation, simply remember your physical body and use your willpower to gently come back to it. As you regain awareness of your body, slowly move your fingers and toes, and then very gently open your eyes with a smile.

The meditation that we have just discussed is a powerful and very effective meditation. It will naturally develop your overall magical faculties, as well as give you a deeper sense of spirituality. It also uses the holy mantra, *Maranatha*, and it is a mantra which has been used for centuries by many holy monks, spiritual seekers, and even the saints. By using the same mantra, you get to share in the divine energy which has accumulated in the mantra for many years. You do not need to be a believer in Christ to benefit from the said mantra. All that you need to do is to know about it and use it regularly.

If you really want to have any real progress in your magical life, then you ought to meditate as often as you can. Many practitioners follow the rule that one should meditate at least twice daily. Instead of being too worried about the number of times that you meditate, you should focus more on having a good-quality meditation session. When it comes to meditation, the best and only way to improve significantly is just like with any other forms of art: continuous practice.

9

Meet Your First Faerie Friend

Now that you have a good understanding of what faeries are and how to acquire the magical mindset (through meditation), it is time to learn just how you can meet your very first faerie friend. The dimension where faeries exist co-exist with our material world. As such, we are not really that separate from one another. Although you cannot see them, you can rest assured that they can see you. In fact, considering the nature of faeries, it is safe to assume that you have been watched by them for so many times in your life already, and you simply did not notice them. The reason why you cannot see them with your physical eyes is because the astral realm has a higher vibration than the gross material world. Therefore, we could not see them, but they could easily see us (because they are coming from a higher vibrational sphere).

So, how do you get to see and meet your first faerie friend? The answer is simple: you should visit their realm, the faerie kingdom. Although they cannot normally be seen by the physical eyes, they can be seen by the eyes of the mind. After all, you are a spirit, and they are also a spirit. In this regard, you are both the same and alike. Not only that, remember that you are more evolved than they are since you are complete with all the four mighty elements of nature while faeries are usually composed of just a single element. Hence, it is within your power to see them and even make friends with them. It is definitely possible, and it is just a matter of knowing what to do and how you do it properly. The key lies in using the mind in a form of free-form meditation. The best way to understand this is through actual practice; hence, without further ado, here are the steps:

Assume a comfortable position and relax. Close your eyes and clear your mind. It is good to meditate for a few minutes to help set the mind in the right state, but this is not always necessary.

Once your mind is clear, imagine that you are in a beautiful place that is full of nature. A good and suggested place to imagine is a forest, but you are also free to imagine yourself in a different place if that is what you prefer.

Spend some time just exploring this beautiful place. As you are walking or moving around this special place, send a message that you would like to meet a faerie in this place. You can do this verbally or even in your mind only together with the help of your willpower. You are in a magical place, so it is very easy to communicate telepathically. While you are in this place, you should also keep your mind open at all times, so that you will know if there is a faerie that might like to connect with you.

Continue your journey in your special place. If a faerie is willing to connect with you, it may appear to you out of nowhere. When this happens, be friendly enough to greet the faerie. If nothing appears, just keep moving around and enjoying the beauty of the place.

Do not force anything to happen. You would not want to influence your mind or whatever happens in this place. Just be open and relax. If no faerie appears at all, you can simply go back to your body and just try again next time. But, most of the time, it would be very easy to find a faerie in this manner.

As soon as you meet a faerie, just connect to it as you would with another human who is likely to be your friend. It is also good to tell the faerie that you mean no harm.

Actually, faeries are very sensitive to energy, which makes them very sensitive as well to the kind of energy that you have in your heart. If there is so much evil in your heart, it would be really hard to have a faerie to reveal itself before you.

Just continue to communicate and make friends with the faerie that appears to you. Do not forget to ask the name of the faerie, so that you can easily call upon it if you ever return to this special place.

After spending a good time with your faerie friend, you can bid him/her farewell and return to your body. To return to your body, simply think of your body and use your willpower to bring your awareness back to it. As soon as you sense your physical body, slowly move your fingers and toes, and very gently open your eyes.

It is important to return to your body very gently to avoid a bad headache. It is also a good practice to write down the name of your new faerie friend on a small sheet of paper that you must keep in secret, especially if the name of your new faerie friend sounds unusual. It is not uncommon for faeries to have quite strange names as compared to most human names.

If you try this technique and nothing seems to happen, do not be discouraged. Just keep practicing, and you will surely meet a faerie soon who could be your friend.

Know that you can always revisit the special place and have quality time with your new faerie friend. In fact, you may also use the name of your faerie friend to call upon it even when you are back in the world of humans. After all, our world and the world of the faeries coexist with each other. Moreover, there is not distance that magical energy could not reach. Everything is connected, so you will never completely lose your connection with your new faerie friend.

Attract Faeries into Your Home

There are certain things that faeries like and are attracted to. After all, they are also living beings with likes and dislikes. By knowing what faeries like, you can attract faeries into your home. This will make having contact with them to be much easier.

A very important thing to note is that faeries like people who have a good heart. Hence, it is encouraged that you develop a kind and loving character. This is good for you, in your life, as well as at having a chance to meet faeries and making them as your friends.

Faeries are also drawn to cheeerful people. I have to admit, I do not have a very cheerful personality. Still, it is more important to have a good heart than just merely being cheerful. But, if you can do both, then that would be better.

Faeries also live plants and herbs, especially roses and rosemaries, as well as ginger. If you have these in your home, there is a good chance that there are already faeries who are living with you at home.

Faeries also love soft and tender music, preferably instrumental music that has a positive feel to it. You can have it playing in the background.

It is also a recommended practice to offer a libation to the faeries. A libation is an offering. Faeries like ginger, milk, strawberry, banana, and bread, but you are also free to make other offerings. I used to offer ginger and some milk every week when I was deep into faerie magic, and I would have to say that it worked really well. When you make an offering and see an animal consuming your libation, do not send the animal away. There are times when faeries may assume physical animal form to receive the offering. Still, most of the time, faeries would not consume the offering physically, but they would receive it on an energy level by appreciating and absorbing the energy of your libation/offering without the need of eating or drinking it physically.

Faeries also love homes that are filled with love, happiness, peace, and laughter. If you have a happy family, then there is a good chance that faeries are already living in your home.

There are many other things that faeries may like. Still, the most important of all is having a good and loving heart. This is not something that goes about by force or something that you can just act out, for faeries are very sensitive and could feel the real quality of energy that you have in your heart. Hence, from now on, do your best to be a good person by making your soul beautiful through the energies of love, peace, compassion, and kindness. This will be good for you and your life, as well as in attracting fairies into your home and/or life.

Faerie Pendulum

The technique that you are about to learn will allow you to make a simple yet effective pendulum that you can use to communicate with faeries. What is a pendulum? It is commonly described as any weighted object suspended on a string/chain that is used in divination.

To make your own pendulum, all that you need is a piece of string and a needle. The length of the string may vary, depending on your personal preference, but it should be long enough to allow the needle to hang freely. Tie one end of the string to the eye of the needle—and you now have a pendulum.

If you are feeling artistic, you can also use a crystal or stone instead of a needle, and then you can use a chain instead of a string. You can also purchase a good-looking pendulum from an occult store.

Now that you have a pendulum, you can use it to communicate with faeries. The first step is to know how your pendulum responds. Take note that a pendulum responds either with a *yes* or *no*. To know how your pendulum responds for a yes, hold the string of your pendulum and allow your pendulum to hang freely. Once your pendulum is still, tell your pendulum, "Show me *yes*." Repeat this statement until your pendulum moves. Your pendulum will swing and move in a particular direction—and this is how your pendulum moves when it means *yes*.

The next step is to know how your pendulum moves to communicate a *no*. The process is the same as for an affirmative answer; but this time, tell your pendulum, "Show me *no*." Your pendulum should move again, but in a different pattern. This will allow you to differentiate it from the *yes* answer.

Now that you know how your pendulum moves for *yes* and for *no*, you are now ready to use your pendulum to communicate with faeries. The steps are as follows:

Hold the pendulum by the chain and let the bob of the pendulum hang freely. Wait until the pendulum is at rest. Once the pendulum is still, invite a faery to come and speak to you. Tell them that you mean them no harm. You can use the following: "If there is a faerie out there, I invite you to please come and speak with me. I do not mean any harm. I come in the spirit of light, love, and peace." Say this thrice. After that, you can ask the pendulum, "Is there a faerie there for me?" Keep silent and see how the pendulum responds. Faeries are naturally magical beings, and they know very well how they can use the pendulum to communicate back to you, if ever they want to.

If you receive a positive response, then that is a good sign that a faerie wants to connect with you. You can now continue your conversation. Feel free to ask the faerie any kind and gentle question, such as, "Do you live in this place?" and "Can we be friends?" and so on.

The pendulum can be a good starting point to build a connection. Once you have established some connection with the faerie already, you can then simply communicate with him/her using telepathy. You can either talk out loud or in your mind only, and then you can receive the messages from your new faery friend telepathically. This is also a good time to ask the name of the fae creature that you are speaking with. You can then use the pendulum as a secondary tool for the purpose of Just be sure to keep your mind open and do not force any response. Be still, relax, and just enjoy the moment.

Once you are done communicating with the faery, ask if you could call on him/her next time. If your faery friend says yes, then you have gained yourself a new friend, indeed. However, if you receive a negative response, do not feel too bad. Just respect the faery for being honest. After this, you can thank the faery and bid him/her farewell. If the faery has given his/her consent, feel free to call upon your faery friend by using his/her name.

Faeries of Avalon

If you ever find yourself in a situation where you need to hide something away from prying eyes, then you can ask help from the faeries of Avalon. These faeries are also the ones who are responsible for hiding the legendary sword of King Arthur from evil. The way to access these faeries is through magical pathworking. The steps are as follows:

Be comfortable and relax. Close your eyes and clear your mind. It is good to start by doing a few minutes of meditation, but this is not necessary. However, if you find your mind bombarded with so many things and thoughts, then it is encouraged that you do not rush the process, and that you spend some time in meditation so as to clear the mind and prepare it for magical work.

Once the mind is clear, see and feel that you are in the legendary place known as Avalon. If you do not know what it is and what the legend is, just keep your mind open and accept however it presents itself to you. But, to help you in visualizing the place, know that Avalon is a body of water that is covered by thick mists. You are going to use the mists to cover and hide whatever it is that you need to keep hidden from prying eyes and from everyone. However, these mists do not follow just anyone. The only way to be able to use these mists is by asking help from the faeries of Avalon, the guardians of this place.

So how do you ask for help from the faeries of Avalon? It should be noted that these faeries are very sensitive, and they would easily be able to feel and read your heart, as well as your intentions. Never come to this place if your heart is full of evil. If there is no goodness in your heart, or if the goodness there be so little, now is the time to walk away because the faeries of Avalon will only work with those who are truly good and of a pure heart.

As soon as you reach Avalon, you will notice that there is nothing much to see except a body of water that is heavily covered by thick mists. Although you may not see them, the faeries of this place are now looking at you.

Talk to the faeries by introducing yourself and assure them that you mean them no harm. Faeries are very cautious of humans since they are well aware of the many evil deeds of mankind.

After introducing yourself, a faerie may come and reveal itself to you. As soon as the faerie appears, just keep quiet and let the faerie direct the conversation. It is also important that you must not appear to be afraid. You are, after all, the magus. You cannot allow faeries to feel superior over you, but you must also be humble at all times.

The faerie will soon ask what you seek; and once you are asked, be very honest about your concern. You will most likely be asked so many questions. Never lie even if the answer might be embarrassing. THe faeries of this place are very sensitive, and they could easily tell what is in your heart and mind. The only reason why they will ask you questions is to make sure that you are honest. It is a test, for they already know all the answers to their questions even before they even ask you anything.

The faerie (or faeries) may grant your request. If your request is granted, you will be given a mist—the mist of avalon. You can then use this mist by imagining the thing (or whatever it may be) that you want to be hidden being covered and shrouded by the legendary mist.

If the faerie does not grant your request, do not get upset. Simply thank the faerie and return to your body. You already know how to return to your body by now. Remember to do it gently.

If the faerie gives you a mist, you can bring it back to the physical world by returning with it. As soon as you return to normal consciousness in our world, see and feel the mist right beside you or in front of you. To cast the mist, simply imagine whatever it is that you wish to be hidden, and then see and feel the mist of avalon covering and shrouding it where no one else could ever see and know about it.

Never underestimate the mist of Avalon. It has proven itself for centuries. Trust in the power of the mist.

Faerie Etiquette

Although not considered strict rules, there are some essential faerie ethics that you should know. Some things that may seem normal to humans may not be normal to faeries. It is good that you become aware of these things to avoid insulting a faerie unintentionally, as you might not have the opportunity to explain yourself.

When you are in the kingdom of the faeries, remember not to eat anything without permission. And, if ever you are given an apple, even if it is completely voluntary, you must never eat it.

If you ever meet the faerie queen, you must not eat anything that she offers you, except if the food or drink is offered during the night. Night and day in faerie land are not the same as ours. Their days can be much longer or much shorter, depending on the specific place in faerie land you find yourself in. Do not worry, it would be very easy to tell if it is day or night by judging the light. If there is much brightness, then it is day; but if it is dark, then you know that it is night. Again, if the faerie queen offers you food or drink during the day, never eat it. In fact, do not even accept it. You can do this by politely refusing the offer, such as by saying, "Thank you, I really appreciate this; however, I could not take it at this time."

If you ever see a faerie ring, regardless of what it is made of, do not enter it. A faerie ring is anything that you may find in faerie land that is in the shape of a ring or circle on the ground. It is believed that there is much power within this ring; however, if you enter it, the faeries of the place will surely punish you. The exception to this is if you are given permission by the faerie queen. Take careful note that it is only the faerie queen who can give you a valid permission. Therefore, if a faerie who is not the queen grants you permission and welcomes you inside the ring, never enter it.

When you are dealing with faeries, it is important to always be kind and gentle. Faeries hate people who are egoistic and evil. Hence, if you currently do not have a nice character, now is the chance for you to make some improvements.

When you enter the faerie realm, never bring a nail (the one used in construction). Faeries hate nails for various reasons. Interestingly, there are also faeries who believe in Jesus Christ. It is said that these faeries hate nails because it reminds them of the suffering and death of the Lord Jesus. The bringing of nails is not just about your existence in the astral, but you must also make sure that your physical body is not in possession of any kind of nail since your astral body (the body that you are using in faerie land) will always be connected to the physical body throughout the journey, and the faeries could sense if your physical body has a nail. It would be to them as if you brought a nail into their kingdom.

Another thing that faeries hate so much is lying. When you deal with faeries, never lie. After all, most faeries have very high sensitivity that they could easily tell if someone is lying. So, never lie to the faeries.

Be sure not to forget these essential faerie ethics. Breaking any of these ethics may result in undesirable consequences, such as causing the faeries to hide from you and even leave you, becoming the subject of a faerie curse, and even to the point where the faeries could continue to cast curses on you (a rare yet possible occurrence).

Bubble Shield

When you work with faeries and/or practice magic, it is always good to learn how to defend yourself from psychic attacks and negative entities. In fact, in some occult schools, psychic self-defense is part of their basic course. Fortunately, it is easy to cast defensive magic as long as you know how to do it properly.

The technique that you are about to learn is a favorite even among advanced practitioners. The reason for this is that it is a basic technique whose power lies in the skills of the caster. Therefore, the more that you grow magically and spiritually, the more powerful this shield is also going to be. Having said that, here are the steps:

Be comfortable and relax. You may close your eyes, if you want, but it is not necessary to do so. Imagine magical energy all around you. Visualizing the universal energy as white light is recommended, but you may also visualize it in any way that you want. The important thing is to know in your mind that it is magical energy that you are imagining.

Next, see and feel that you are drawing the universal energy toward you and have it form into a shield like a bubble around you. Know that this is your bubble shield, and it protects you from all psychic attacks and from all negative energies.

The next step is to make your bubble shield strong and powerful so as to increase its effectiveness. The way to do this is by pouring more energy into it. To do this, continue drawing energy from the universe and keep pouring it into your bubble shield. As you are doing this, you should be able to see (in your imagination) your shield shining brighter and brighter. You should also be able to feel the power of your shield as it gets stronger and stronger. Take as much time as you may need. Do not rush this part of the process. On average, this usually takes about two minutes, but some practitioners even spend as much as five to ten minutes. There are no strict rules, so just be sure to charge your bubble shield with as much energy as it can contain. Keep the energy concentrated and intact. You should be able to see and feel your bubble shield coming to life at this point.

Once you are happy with the power of your shield, you can stop pouring energy into it. You can now conclude the technique by saying an affirmation to further impress upon your shield its task, such as by telling your shield, "You protect me from all negative energies and psychic attacks."

Now that your shield is cast, you can now go about your day knowing that you have a bubble shield that protects you.

It should be noted that psychic shields require energy for them to continuously exist and perform their functions. On average, a shield created in the manner as described would last for about seven hours, depending on how much negative energies it is exposed to. However, as you gain more experience and develop your skills, the lifespan of your shield will also increase.

You are free to cast the bubble shield as often as you like. It is recommended to use it before you journey into the faerie land or whenever you feel at risk. This shield is not limited to faerie encounters but also has other practical purposes. It is also often used when you know that you will be exposed to various people or whenever you find yourself in a difficult situation. Once you get used to casting this shield, you can even cast it quickly at any time, and even in public without being noticed by anyone.

Meet the Elemental Guardian Faeries

There are faeries whose task in life is to guard and look after their respective element to maintain balance in the universe. Needless to say, these faeries are very knowledgeable when it comes to the element that they belong to.

The technique that you are about to learn will allow you to enter into the world of the elements and meet the guardian faeries therein. If you get lucky and manage to build a bond of friendship with these beings, you will surely learn a lot from them as they are very knowledgeable in the craft of magic, especially with respect to their respective element. Here are the steps:

Assume a comfortable position and relax. Close your eyes and free your mind. Relax and drift into nothingness—a nothingness where everything is possible, just as the universe came out from nothing. This is the mystery of the void, which is true power within.

You are about to meet the guardian faeries of the Earth element. Imagine a rich and beautiful forest right in front of you. Enter this forest and explore it.

As you walk, you find a clearing, and in this empty clearing, stands the guardian faerie. What does it look like? Is it male or female? Faeries can take any form that they want, so do not be deceived by the way they appear to you. They may take the form of an animal or even a human child. It is the spirit that matters, not the shell that covers it.

Approach the guardian faerie gently and introduce yourself. From here, proceed as you would when meeting a faerie for the first time. Do not forget to ask for the name of the guardian faerie that appears to you. Enjoy the conversation and the moment that you now have with the guardian earth faery.

At any time that you want to end this meditation, thank the guardian faerie and bid them farewell. You can then gently return to your body. Although not necessary, it is also a good practice to write in a notebook whatever has happened in your magical journey so that you will not forget about it. It is also a good way to note down the name of the faerie that may appear before you. Just be sure to keep your notebook private and hide it away from prying eyes.

The same technique applies when meeting the guardian faeries of the other elements. You simply have to go to their territory and meet the guardian of that place. Hence, if you want to meet the water guardian faery, see and feel that you are in a vast ocean. If you want to meet the fire guardian faerie, see and feel that you are in the center of a great sun. If you want to meet the air guardian faerie, see and feel that you are flying in the sky.

The key is to expose yourself to the place or territory of the element concerned. Once you are within the territory of the element, then you can easily meet the beings and guardians of that place. Be open, always be kind, enjoy the journey, and keep on learning.

Faerie Circle Dance Song

If you ever find yourself invited or participating in the faery circle dance, then you must dance—dance with them. It is a dance that moves in a circular fashion, with a strange magical music in the background as if to put you deeper and deeper into a trance.

The faerie circle dance is a mystical dance that will imbue you with so much magic. It is not uncommon to receive spiritual realizations during this dance, as well as attaining a significant development in your magical-spiritual level.

If you ever find yourself invited or participating in this mysterious dance in faeryland, remember to keep your mind open. Stop thinking and rationalizing things. This mystical dance is not meant to be understood by the mind, but it should be felt with the heart and soul.

Simply follow the faeries by copying them. Let go and stop thinking. Soon enough, as you adjust with the energy of the dance, you will be dancing on your own, flowing with the natural rhythm—and this is how you shall experience the real power and energy of the ancient, sacred, and magical dance.

Building a Deeper Friendship with the Faeries

When it comes to building a stronger bond of friendship with the fae creatures, it is important to be sincere. Sincerity which also equates to honesty is held by the faeries of a high esteem, and it is absolutely necessary if you want to have a good relationship with faeries.

As you may have noticed, I have told you to always get the name of the faery whom you encounter while on a magical journey. This is because you can easily reconnect with the faery by using their name. In magic, it has long been established that names have power, and names can serve as a connection that links between two or more individuals. As such, you can use the name of the faery (and the memory that you have with them) to reconnect with the said faery.

However, it is important to note that you will not use the name of a faery to manipulate them or make them submit by force or pressure to whatever you desire. It is not a good idea to mess with the faeries for they can also be very powerful, and you would not want to engage into a magical battle with these magical creatures.

The right way to use the name of the faery is for reconnecting with them. To do this, you can return to the place where you have met the faery, and then simply call out its name. If it wants to reconnect with you, then it shall reappear just like what happened when you first met each other. However, if the faery does not reappear, it may be because it no longer wants to communicate with you or perhaps they are just busy or unavailable at the moment. You can simply come back some other time and try again. It will be obvious if the faery simply does not want to reconnect with you anymore if it has not appeared to you after about five attempts. In this case, if this ever happens, just let it go and find another faery who can be your real friend.

But, if the faery reappears, then you can have another moment of bonding—and if you both enjoy each other's company, then there is a good chance that you will have more meetings and fun moments together. This is the way to strengthen and deepen your friendship with a faery. It is very much similar to building a deeper connection and relationship with another human being.

You can also invite the faery to come into our world. To do this, close your eyes and imagine the faery with whom you want to connect to. Imagine and re-experience the moment that you have shared with them. This way, you will be more connected to the faery. After re-establishing the connection in your mind, call out the name of your faerie friend, and add a request that they come to you, such as by saying, "(Name of the faerie), please come and visit me now." Say this at least thrice as you imagine the face of the faerie, and say it as if you were directly talking to the said faerie.

After calling out to the faerie as aforesaid, pause for a while and just relax. Keep your eyes closed and your mind open. Just wait and give it some time for the faery to appear to you. If it wants to reconnect, then you can enjoy another moment of bonding with them; but if not, feel free to try again some other time or until it becomes clear that the faerie simply no longer wants to connect with you.

Do not worry, there are many faeries out there who are very friendly and would also like to have a good friendship with a human, especially with someone who practices magic such as yourself.

Developing Clairvoyance

Although not necessary, it is still good and recommended to develop the power of clairvoyance when you work with faeries. What is the power of clairvoyance? Clairvoyance means *clear-seeing*. If you develop this ability, you will be able to see your faery friends more clearly and easily. It will also allow you to make your magical journeys to be more vivid and real, which would make the experience significantly more powerful.

The good news is that with the right practice, it is very easy to develop this ability. The technique that you are about to learn has been used by witches for centuries to develop the power of clairvoyance. It also uses the power of the fire element—the element that governs the power of magical sight. Here are the steps:

For this technique, you will need to light a candle. Position the candle in front of you. You may do this exercise while sitting or standing or even while lying down. The important thing is to be able to stare at the flame of the candle comfortably.

Look at the flame of the candle and gently focus on it. Do not think about anything. If thoughts arise in the mind, ignore them. Only focus ever so gently on the flame. Relax and let go of everything else.

Continue this exercise for as long as you like. At any time that you want to end this exercise, gently and slowly bring your awareness back to your body, slowly move your fingers and toes, and gently open your eyes.

As you can see, the steps are very simple and straightforward. The fire element will automatically trigger and strengthen the ajna chakra (the third eye chakra located between the eyebrows). The ajna chakra is the energy center that governs the power of clairvoyance.

It should also be noted that regular practice of the said exercise will also naturally and significantly develop your overall psychic abilities and senses, as well as give you a deeper realization of spirituality. It is recommended to practice this exercise at least once daily. Since you will be using a lighted candle, be sure to observe all necessary cautions concerning the physical world for safety.

Agatha the Ocean Faerie

Since you will be dealing with faerie magick, it is good to get to know the Ocean faerie named Agatha. Agatha is a very friendly faerie who still has not lost hope in humanity. She has existed for centuries, so you can rest assured that she has rich knowledge and wisdom pertaining to the magical arts. To meet this very interesting faerie, you should visit the celestial ocean known as *Oceanus*.

To reach Oceanus, you need to travel with your mind. Oceanus exists in the astral dimension. Are you ready to go to this beautiful and magical place? If yes, then here are the steps:

Be comfortable and relax. Close your eyes and free your mind. Names have power. By conjuring the name, you can use it to create a connection to what the name represents. Now, in line with this magical principle, say the name of the magical place slowly and repeatedly in your mind: *Oceanus... Oceanus... Oceanus...*

As you say the name of the place, also exercise your willpower to be there. You will soon be transported into this special place. Do you see the might and beauty of the ocean? Since you are in meta-astral form, you would not have to worry even going underwater. Go deep into the blue water and explore the Kingdom of Oceanus. You might be able to find mermaids and interesting sea creatures here as well. For now, do not engage in any form of conversation except for a pleasant and gentle greeting.

Try to look for the big green fish. It is the fish that would lead you to Agatha. This fish is always swimming in circles around the kingdom. Once you find the fish, follow it.

As you follow the fish, you will soon be led to a big golden shell. This is the home of Faerie Agatha. As soon as you find the golden shell, go to it, and knock.

If Agatha is there, she would surely be pleased to see you. If the shell does not open, just come back to it some other time.

If you ever see Agatha, introduce yourself and tell her your purpose for visiting. You do not need to have a very deep purpose. Simply admitting the fact that you want to be friends with her would be enough.

Enjoy the moment with the Faerie Agatha. She might even tour you around the kingdom and introduce you to some friends—and she has so many friends. Feel free to ask her questions and talk to her about anything.

To end the journey, thank the Faerie Agatha and bid her farewell. You can then gently return to your body using the usual steps. Know that you can always visit this wonderful and magical kingdom, and that Faerie Agatha will always be there to listen to you.

Meet Your Faerie Self

It is believed that those who engage in faerie magic are actually the ones who have a fae personality. There are even those who believe that they are 100% faerie who just happen to possess a human body. Regardless of what you think of yourself in terms of being part fairy or whole fairy, you can meet yourself, and you can more clearly tell who you truly are. The steps are as follows:

Assume a comfortable position and relax. Close your eyes and free the mind. You are about to meet your fairy self—the self within the self. You might want to do a few minutes of meditation to prepare for this encounter.

Once your mind is clear, say, "I desire to meet my fairy self." Say this thrice. As you do, focus on the words and use your willpower to conjure your faerie self.

What do you see? If something appears, then it must be your faerie self. If nothing appears, you can simply try again some other time. It is only either perhaps you are not ready yet to meet your faerie self or you simply do not have a faery self at all, which means that no part of you is faery.

Now, if something appears, gently focus on it. Do not judge anything. Just be a passive observer. You should also avoid getting too excited as this will only pull you back into your body and prevent whatever revelation that could take place. Just stay calm and relaxed.

Talk to your faerie self. Feel free to ask questions and everything that you would like to know. Never forget that your faery self is you. If it happens to be really good and magical, it is only because there is goodness and magic in you. Many times, we just fail to let the magic out to shine. But, this conversation and meeting that you now have with your faery self is an assurance that, indeed, there is so much magic in you—for a part of you is a faery.

Enjoy this moment with your faery self. At any time that you want to end this meeting, thank your faery self, and then gently return to your body.

You just had a meeting with your magical faery self. If you think that you have just met an awesome being, it is only because you are awesome. Now, let that beauty and power shine. Be you, and be free.

Developing Love and Kindness

If you want to develop more love and kindness, then you can use this powerful meditation. This meditation is based on the teachings of Grandmaster Choa Kok Sui. It is a simplified version of the Twin Hearts meditation. With this meditation and magical technique, you will bless the Earth and all those of the Earth with the pure energy of love and kindness. Love and kindness energy is always pure and holy. Here are the steps:

Assume a comfortable position and relax. Close your eyes and free the mind. Position your hands in the manner of giving a blessing, palms facing outward. Now, imagine the Earth floating in front of you, the size of a small ball.

You are going to bless the Earth with love and kindness. In the process, you will also be blessed and filled with the divine energy of love and kindness.

Think of a happy memory. Re-experience this happy memory in your mind as if it were happening for the first time. You are joyful and full of peace and love. This will conjure a boost of positive energy within you. Allow this energy to spread from your heart, then to your arms, and out through your hands, and then pour and share that energy with the Earth that is floating in front of you, thereby blessing the Earth with pure love and kindness.

You can also think of other happy memories to keep the energy flowing. Keep pouring energy to the Earth, blessing it and everyone in it with love and kindness. Imagine that you are also blessing your family and loved ones with the energy of love and kindness. See and feel the Earth in front of you lighting up and shining brightly as you bathe it in the energy of compassion (love and kindness).

At any time that you want to end this meditation, slowly return to your body, and cease all thoughts. Gently focus on your breath for some time. Nothing must exist in the mind but the breath. Be one with this breath for breath is life, and then very slowly open your eyes to meet the world.

Faeries Everywhere

Faeries may be found everywhere because our worlds coexist with each other. By simply being open to faeries and welcoming them into your life, you can significantly increase the chances of meeting them. A good technique to use is to close your eyes and see with your mind whenever you feel like there might be a faerie in a place. Keep your mind open and reach out to the spirits in the place. You can easily do this by closing your eyes, keeping it clear, and asking, "Is there a faery in this place?" If you sense the presence of a faery, you can say, "Please reveal yourself to me," or "Make yourself known."

Keep your mind open, and do not try to influence or control anything. Faeries usually communicate telepathically, so it is important to keep your mind clear and still. When it comes to clearing and stilling the mind, regular practice of meditation is strongly encouraged.

From now on, be more open to faeries and get used to seeing with your mind's eye. There are fairies everywhere; and if you just open your heart to them, they would gladly fill it with love, joy, peace, and magic.

Faery Beam of Light

The faery beam of light is a magical technique that anyone can learn. It involves sending positive energy to someone. It is an easy spell to learn and yet it can be very helpful for someone in need. Here are the steps:

Relax as much as you can. When you are manipulating magical life energy, it is important to be as relaxed as possible. Take note that manipulation of magical energy is not about the use of force, but it relies more on harmony.

According to Hermetic Occult Science, the left eye is receptive. This means that you can send energy to another through their left eye. It is a channel through which you could penetrate their psyche. We are going to take advantage of that magical fact in this exercise. The steps are as follows:

Choose a subject to whom you want to send positive energy to. It is preferable that the subject is someone who is within your range of vision; however, if this is not possible, you can still use this technique by imagining the subject standing right in front of you.

Imagine feeling the energy that you want to send to your subject within you. For example, if you want to send the energy of happiness, then feel happiness within you. After all, we can only give that which we have. To evoke the feeling of happiness, you might want to remember a happy memory. Even a completely made-up memory will also work. The important thing is to evoke the desired quality of energy within you.

Once you have the desired energy present within you, the next step is to send that energy to your subject. To do this, see and feel that you are sending a beam of light coming from your eyes toward the left eye of your subject. See and feel that you are continuously sending this energy from your eyes into your subject's left eye where it shall enter the subject and then fill their psyche (soul).

Gradually see your subject getting filled with the energy that you are sending. Continue accumulating the energy in their soul until they are shining brightly with the energy that you are sending to them. Continue for as long as may be necessary; after which, you may stop and just wait for the spell to manifest.

It usually takes some time for spells to manifest because it has to travel through various planes of existence before physical manifestation can be achieved. Hence, after sending the energy, just stop and be patient, knowing that the magic is now at work.

Maintain a High Vibration

Maintaining a high vibration will significantly increase your chances of a faerie encounter. This is because faeries like people who have a high vibration. But, what does it mean to have a high vibration, and how can you achieve it?

It should be noted that having a high vibration depends on the quality of energy that is present. Positive energy qualities like love, goodness, gentleness, and peace are considered energies of high vibrational frequency, while negative energies like anger, fear, worry, stress, and sadness are vibrating at a low frequency. Good faeries are drawn to high-energy vibrations and stay away from low-energy vibrations.

It also follows that if you want to have a high vibration, then it is as easy and simple as filling your mind with positive energy qualities—positive thoughts.

By keeping your heart and mind good and pure, you can have and maintain a high vibration. It should also be noted that this can be maintained regardless of what happens around you. Even in a difficult situation, you can maintain your peace of mind, as well as the goodness in your heart. This is another reason why it is encouraged that you work on improving yourself by being a truly good human being. Love and kindness have a magic of their own that transcends all human logic and suffering. Indeed, love conquers all.

It should also be noted that having a high vibration is a natural and effective psychic self-defense. The reason for this is that once you are vibrating at a higher energy frequency, you will be above the energies (negative energies) that are vibrating at a lower frequency; hence, they could not touch you. Even if curses are hurled against you, you will not be harmed for they could not even reach you. This is another benefit of being good and pure.

It may not always be easy to be vibrating at a high frequency because the world can really be a difficult place to live in. There are people who are good at messing things up and could really test your patience and virtue. This is something that you must learn to overcome; otherwise, you will be controlled by the world. Through the practice of meditation, you can learn to master your mind and be free from the bondage of the external world. Keep practicing, and you will surely reap the benefits soon.

A Sacred Call

I hope that you have enjoyed reading this book. Our humble journey ends here. But, before I let you go, there is something that I want to share with you. I have been practicing witchcraft for more than 20 years, and I am now a follower of Jesus Christ. It is interesting to know that many witches and wizards these days are also turning to Christ for genuine spirituality and for more magic.

Shortly after Christ was born, He was visited by the three magi, which some people these days refer to as the three wise men. Based on the original text, the word *magi* was used. The word *magi* is the plural of the word *magus*—and the word *magus* is where the word *magic* came from. Hence, Jesus was visited by three magical practitioners. The church does not want to talk about it and even tried to change the word into *wise men* or even the *three kings* as if to hide its real meaning. But, indeed, three magical practitioners came after Jesus was born.

In my life, despite all the magic and rituals that I have learned, I came to a point of complete darkness and depression. My magic could not save me. That was the time when Jesus came and rescued me. I have been serving Him since then.

I would like to ask my dear reader to kindly give Christ a chance in your life. Forget about what you think you know about Him from what you have learned from religion. You can start with a clean slate, and get to know Him on your own. In this regard, I highly suggest starting out by reading the Bible. No, you do not need to read the whole Bible. You can easily start by reading the *Book of Matthew*, which also happens to be the first book in the New Testament of the Bible. This is a good way to know about the life and teachings of Jesus Christ. Do not worry, it is not a long book. In fact, I managed to finish reading it in just one sitting. Just please give it a try and see how it works for you.

Unlike other gods out there who do not care about you and would require a complicated ritual before they pay attention to you, Jesus is always with you, and He loves you. In fact, He loves you so much that He already suffered and died for you, so that you can enjoy salvation with Him in paradise.

I sincerely hope that you may give Christ a chance. He might just change your life forever.

With light and love, Blessed Be!

Don't miss out!

Visit the website below and you can sign up to receive emails whenever Merryl Kowalska publishes a new book. There's no charge and no obligation.

https://books2read.com/r/B-A-OMZV-TINDC

BOOKS 2 READ

Connecting independent readers to independent writers.

Did you love *Faerie Magick for Beginners*? Then you should read *Solitary Witchcraft for Beginners*[1] by Merryl Kowalska!

[2]

Immersive Magic: Solitary Witchcraft for Beginners is an occult codex that teaches the ways of magic. It is written for new magical practitioners and those who want to start on a magical journey. It is also designed for solitary practice, which means that you can actually start experiencing a magical life completely on your own and without any external help. Hence, nothing can stop you.

Immersive Magic: Solitary Witchcraft for Beginners reveals the essential teachings and practices of witchcraft. It is also

---

1. https://books2read.com/u/mZE1e2

2. https://books2read.com/u/mZE1e2

written in a simple, direct, and easy-to-understand format, so that you can easily focus on learning and experiencing the magical life. This book will initiate you into the art of witchcraft. You will learn the right ancient knowledge, and you will be equipped with the right practices, so that you can truly experience what it truly means to live a magical life, and not just know it on an intellectual level. After all, true witchcraft is meant to be lived and experienced on a deep and personal level.

Another benefit of solitary witchcraft is that you do not need to follow rules that you do not like. You can enjoy so much more freedom and even exercise your creativity. It will not force you to do these that you would rather not engage in. Indeed, if you are looking for a magical and spiritual path that will allow you to enjoy so much freedom, then you would not go wrong with the solitary witchcraft approach.

It should be noted that solitary witchcraft does not mean that you are completely alone. Once you reach a deeper understanding of the universe, you will realize that you are, in fact, never alone. The energy of the universe keeps on flowing, and you are actually one with all things. Solitary witchcraft is not about being alone, but it is simply not being part of a formal and strict group or tradition. It is about being free and being who you truly are. It is about self-expression and absolute exercise of freewill. It is also about wonder and art. Indeed, there is so much that this path has to offer, but the question is: Are you ready for it? Do you have the courage to walk where angels fear to tread?

If you feel an inner voice or calling within you, or if you feel a desire within for magic and spirituality, then come, and we shall take this path together, to behold and embrace the path of solitary witchcraft.

Also by Merryl Kowalska

Immersive Magic
A Guide to Acquiring an Astral Magic Wand
Solitary Witchcraft for Beginners
Faerie Magick for Beginners

www.ingramcontent.com/pod-product-compliance
Lightning Source LLC
Chambersburg PA
CBHW031421160726
47993CB00003B/1335